Fabulous Physics

Five Amazing Stories of People Who Solved Nature's Puzzles

Nury Vittachi

Illustrations by Step Cheung

Contents

THE MAN WHO SAW A LIVING SKELETON

WILHELM RONTGEN WAS A QUIET MAN, teaching science at a university.

But there was one thing special about him — he had a lot of patience, and would try and try again to achieve what he wanted to achieve, never giving up.

When he had been a teenage boy in Germany in 1865, he wanted to go to university but did not have the right qualifications. So instead, he got into a polytechnic when he was 19, and studied really hard.

Young Wilhelm was a patient person, and would try and try again, however long it took, to achieve what he wanted to achieve.

This was a good way to be. He did so well that 10 years later he was a professor at a university himself.

STEP C.

After that, every year was the same. He gave lectures for part of the week and did experiments for part of the week, because he wanted to make his own scientific discovery, not just spend his life teaching people about the findings of other scientists.

He did this right through his 30s, and then right through his 40s.

But he discovered nothing new.

By the time he was 50 years old, most people in his position would have stopped being ambitious. They would have been happy enough to be old professors, ready for retirement.

But not Wilhelm Rontgen. He kept doing experiments, never giving up.

One night, he was experimenting with vacuum tubes, which are glass tubes filled with electrified gas.

When he turned the lights off to see if the tube was glowing, he noticed a light shining on a work bench away from the desk. How odd!

He switched his experimental tube on and off a few times, but could still see something glowing on the bench.

In the dark, he lit a match to provide light, and walked over to the bench. A piece of cardboard with a chemical on it was glowing.

Rontgen realized that invisible rays were coming out of the tubes and crossing the room, somehow causing this chemical to glow.

He started doing experiments with these unknown rays, which he called X-rays, and learned strange things about them: they seemed to be able to go through solid surfaces. They could go through glass, or wood — or even skin.

Excited, he ate and slept in his laboratory so that he could do more experiments and learn more about these mysterious rays.

One day soon afterwards, he asked his wife Anna to hold up her hand, and he took a picture of it using X-rays. The picture showed a skeleton hand!

Anna gasped: "I have seen my own death!"

When Rontgen's discovery was shown to the world, he became famous. He was given the very first Nobel Prize in Physics.

Today, machines based around his discovery of X-rays are used on most people at some time in their lives. Doctors use them to save the lives of patients.

And he also inspired Marie Curie, who we will meet in the next story.

But maybe Wilhelm Rontgen should really be remembered for his patience — the man who would never give up!

THE SERVANT GIRL WHO BEAT EINSTEIN

THE POOR YOUNG WOMAN who worked as a domestic helper looking after children on a farm seemed destined to achieve nothing special in her life.

She was in her early 20s, but had already suffered a hard life.

Maria Sklodowska's mother had died when she was just 10 years old.

And her father was a science teacher who lost his job when he went on a protest calling for his small country, Poland, to be independent. It was governed at the time by Russia, a much bigger country.

Maria's dad was too poor to pay for education for his children but he gave them the one thing he had: a love of science.

STEP C.

The two girls in the family came up with a plan. The younger one would earn money working as a domestic helper looking after children, and the older one would study.

Then, after two years, the older one, who hopefully would have a job and an income by then, would help the younger one, who could then study.

And so young Maria ended up looking after the children of a farmer.

The sisters' plan worked, keeping them both happy and occupied.

After two years, Maria left the farm and went to Paris to study science, remembering the marvelous things that her father had taught her. She changed her name slightly to Marie, which sounded more French.

One day, she went to visit a laboratory-for-hire because she needed a place to do her experiments — and met a handsome bearded Frenchman, who was the boss of the lab.

This man, Pierre Curie, fell in love with her, and they soon got married.

Her name was now Marie Curie. She read a science journal which said that a scientist named Wilhelm Rontgen (who we met in the previous story) had found amazing invisible rays coming out of a certain type of rock. He called them X-rays.

Invisible rays! What on earth could they be? She decided that she would work out what they were, and find out if other substances gave out invisible rays.

For months, she and her husband worked on the challenge.

They arranged for a cart pulled by a horse to bring a huge variety of substances to their lab so they could be tested to see if they gave out invisible rays.

Two great achievements followed. First, she discovered a substance, radium, that gave out more invisible rays than had ever been measured before. And second, she thought of a good name for this new area of science: "radioactivity".

Invisible rays had a lot of practical uses, especially in detecting broken bones.

Years later, Marie and her daughter organized X-ray units to be taken out to the places where soldiers were fighting in World War I and they saved many lives. They also discovered that radiation could be used to kill the disease called cancer.

Marie was given TWO Nobel Prizes, and became friends with Einstein.

But one thing they didn't know in those days was that if a person spent a lot of time near radioactive machines it would make that person sick.

She died in 1934, aged 66, probably from having spent so much time near X-ray machines.

But she remains the most famous female scientist in history — not bad for a girl whose first job was working as a domestic helper for the children of a farmer.

THE BOY WHO CLIMBED TO THE TOP

A LONG TIME AGO, a man living in India had a dream. He saw his tiny son, Abdus Salam, climbing a tree.

"Be careful," the worried father called out.

The little boy, hardly pausing on his upward journey, shouted down: "Don't worry, Dad. I know what I'm doing."

The small child climbed higher and higher, and eventually clambered right out of sight, lost in the clouds.

The dream ended. The man woke up and went to give his sleeping child a kiss.

Little Abdus Salam was a very smart child, and at a young age was reading books in different languages and doing mathematics for fun. He lived in a very poor part of India called Jhang, which is now in Pakistan. His parents valued education and encouraged him to continue to learn.

When the boy reached the age of 14, he sat for the university entrance exam and managed to get in.

The boy's father was very proud. He believed that his son could do anything. But what should his job be, after he graduated while still a teenager? In those days, the 1940s, the highest achievement the dad could think of was for his son to get a job working for the then Indian Railways.

But things did not go well. For a start, the boy had spent a lot of time staying up late at night reading, which meant that he wore glasses — so his eyesight was considered a problem. Then they discovered that there were rules about how old you had to be to join the railways, and Abdus Salam was too young.

So his brilliance had made him a failure.

Life was so unfair!

Disappointed, the boy went back to university to do what he knew he could do: studying books. It turned out to be the right move. He managed to win a scholarship to study at another university — Cambridge in the UK.

Have you heard of Cambridge? It's one of world's top universities. Abdus Salam travelled to the UK and found that he fitted like a glove among the thinkers at the university city.

He became a top scientist, although he kept his love of Asian culture. When he met Albert Einstein, Abdus Salam talked to him about eastern views of God and religion, and Einstein was fascinated, finding interesting parallels between what he heard and what was being discussed by the quantum physics community.

Back in India, the boy's father missed his son, of course, but he soon saw Abdus Salam's face again. It was in newspapers around the world when the boy from a poor part of Pakistan won the Nobel Prize.

The dad also realized that the dream that he had had many years ago had come true, in a metaphorical way.

His boy had climbed a tall tree, causing worries for his parents, and had eventually climbed right out of sight.

And he remembered the child's words in the dream: "Don't worry, Dad. I know what I'm doing."

THE QUIET QUEEN OF PHYSICS

A TEENAGE GIRL HAD A PROBLEM. Her parents were among the few in China who believed that girls should be educated, and she had won a position in The Normal School — a place which was anything but normal. It was a famous boarding school near Shanghai, specializing in art and literature.

But the problem was this: the thing that the girl, Wu Chien-Shiung, really loved, was science, which was a Boy Subject. Girls were not allowed to study it.

So, after a full day at school, she would work in the evenings, as the stars came out, on books on physics and chemistry.

Still, there's nothing teachers love more than to see students who really want to learn — so they quietly encouraged her, and she eventually ended up studying physics at a university in China.

It may be that she worked harder than her classmates, to prove that women could study subjects men thought were too difficult for them.

Her professors told the ambitious, hardworking young woman that all the top work in physics in those days, the 1930s, was happening not in China, but in the West. So Wu Chien-Shiung got on a boat and sailed to the USA.

Even there, women scientists were rare. Still, she was hard-working and reliable and willing to play a secondary role, staying in the background.

She did much of the experimental work for two male scientists, Lee Tsung-Dao and Yang Chen-Ning, who were given the Nobel Prize for the resulting discoveries.

During World War II, she worked on a secret assignment to create the first atom bomb, but that project is associated with famous male scientists.

In fact, her career can be summed up like this: "It's amazing what you can achieve if you don't mind who gets the credit!"

There was one sad thing in her life: China went through a period of upheaval and unrest from the war until the 1970s, and scientists were blacklisted so she was never able to go back and visit her family.

But she loved her work, and as the years went by, she became famous herself in the world of science. Some people called her "The First Lady of Physics", while others addressed her as "Madame Wu". In 1975, she was elected the first female President of the American Physical Society.

When she died in 1997, her ashes were taken to be sprinkled at the primary school in China where she first studied.

But before that, she'd become the first living scientist to have an asteroid named after her. So, if you also like to read science books at night, like she did, look out of the window and point a telescope at the night sky.

Perhaps you might see a tiny light travelling past — one which bears the name 2752 Wu Chien-Shiung, named after the girl who studied late at night as the stars came out.

THE BOY WHO SECRETLY READ THE BOOKS HE WAS BINDING

A BOY AGED 14 HAD a mind full of questions — but nowhere to find answers. He came from a poor family in the UK, and they did not have enough money to send him to school, let alone university.

When they ran out of cash to buy food to eat, they told the boy, whose name was Michael Faraday, to go out to work to learn a trade and earn money.

At the age of 14, he got a job for a man who hand-made books and ran a small bookshop.

This turned out to be a great place for Michael. He was surrounded by knowledge, and could secretly read the books as he worked on binding their pages together.

One of the books he read was about science — and he quickly fell in love with the subject. After that, he didn't just skim the books, but taught himself science.

After he reached the age of 20, he started going to science lectures in London. This was the year 1812. At one of these, he made friends with a top scientist who was impressed by the attitude and knowledge of the young man who had not been to school or university.

When the scientist's servant fell ill just before a trip, Michael was given the job.

But it was an unhappy time. The scientist's wife was one of those people who believe that servants and masters should be kept strictly separate, so poor Michael lived very humbly, had to sit outside the carriage even on cold, wet days, and had to eat separately from his boss. So there was no time for scientific discussions.

But eventually Michael did become an assistant scientist — and started making a huge number of discoveries himself.

He had a natural talent for it, and made finding after finding, becoming famous.

In fact, he eventually made so many scientific breakthroughs that the other scientists wanted to make him president of the Royal

Society, which was a club for the world's top scientists.

He refused. Because of his humble background, he said that he didn't want that sort of fame. Instead, he volunteered for humble duties at the church to which he belonged.

In his lab, he discovered lots of things that no one had ever noticed before, particularly with regard to electricity and magnetism and chemistry.

Michael Faraday is much admired by scientists for the way he used his love of knowledge to get over the barriers of being poor and uneducated.

Maybe his greatest invention was finding a way to use electricity to create movement in machines. This was the foundation of the electric motor.

Now if you think of all the objects around you that use electricity for power — cars, vacuum cleaners, electric toothbrushes, spaceships and almost every other device of technology — then you can see just how much he contributed.

Pretty amazing for a boy who only managed to get hold of books by sewing bindings on them!

Albert Einstein was stunned by how Michael Faraday combined a world-changing level of scientific genius with a gentle, spiritual humbleness, and kept a picture of him in his study.

KEEP READING

READING ABOUT THE LIVES of scientists and other discoverers adds to our store of knowledge, but we hope also leads us towards something much greater, which is wisdom.

This book is part of a series, which we hope you'll enjoy reading, and will spur you on to do your own scientific research.

The creators of this book wish you success in your explorations.

THE YOUNG SCIENTISTS SERIES

Book 1: SECRETS IN THE ROCKS
Five Astounding Tales of People Solving Mysteries Beneath Our Feet

Book 2: FABULOUS PHYSICS
Five Amazing Stories of People Who Solved Nature's Puzzles

Book 3: MAGICAL MATHEMATICS
Five Astonishing Stories of People Who Did Miracles with Numbers

Book 4: BREAKERS OF BARRIERS
Five Stunning Stories of People Demolishing Walls to Make History

Book 5: SCIENTIFIC PIONEERS
Five Incredible Tales of People Who Helped Develop the Scientific Method

Book 6: THE AMAZING QUANTUM
Five Awesome Stories of People Who Made a Revolution in Physics

Book 7: THE SCIENCE OF HUMANITY
Five Fascinating Stories of People Who Helped Us Understand Ourselves

Book 8: WOMEN OF DISCOVERY
Five Super Stories of Fabulous Females Who Made Scientific History

Book 9: THE INVENTOR'S SPARK
Five Marvelous Stories of People Who Helped Shape the Modern World

Book 10: ADVANCES IN ALCHEMY
Five Startling Stories of Chemistry and Biology

Book 11: THE CALL OF THE STARS
Five Wonderful Stories of People Looking to the Heavens

Book 12: MYSTERIES OF NATURE'S LAWS
Five Striking Stories of People Investigating the Deepest Puzzles of Reality

Published by

WS Education, an imprint of
World Scientific Publishing Co. Pte. Ltd.
5 Toh Tuck Link, Singapore 596224
USA office: 27 Warren Street, Suite 401-402, Hackensack, NJ 07601
UK office: 57 Shelton Street, Covent Garden, London WC2H 9HE

National Library Board, Singapore Cataloguing in Publication Data
Name(s): Vittachi, Nury, 1958– | Cheung, Step, illustrator.
Title: Fabulous physics : five amazing stories of people who solved nature's puzzles / author, Nury Vittachi ; illustrator, Step Cheung.
Other title(s): Young scientists series ; 2.
Description: Singapore : World Scientific Publishing Co Pte Ltd, 2017.
Identifier(s): OCN 969702656 | ISBN 978-981-3221-36-9 (paperback)
Subject(s): LCSH: Physicists--Juvenile literature. | Scientists--Juvenile literature. | Physics--Juvenile literature. | Science--Juvenile literature.
Classification: DDC 530.0922--dc23

British Library Cataloguing-in-Publication Data
A catalogue record for this book is available from the British Library.

All royalties received will be channelled to the National Book Development Council of Singapore (NBDCS) as a gift from the author.

First published 2017
Reprinted 2018

Printed in Singapore